Puzzlers:
Lateral Thinking Puzzles

10 9 8 7 6 5 4 3 2 1

Published by Sterling Publishing Company, Inc.
387 Park Avenue South, New York, N.Y. 10016

Material in this collection was adapted from
Ingenious Lateral Thinking Puzzles © Paul Sloane and Des MacHale
Perplexing Lateral Thinking Puzzles © Paul Sloane and Des MacHale

Distributed in Canada by Sterling Piublishing
c/o Canadian Manda Group, One Atlantic Avenue, Suite 105
Toronto, Ontario, Canada M6K 3E7
Distributed in Australia by Capricorn Link (Australia) Pty Ltd
P.O. Box 6651, Baulkham Hills, Business Centre, NSW 2153, Australia
Manufactured in the United States of America.

Sterling ISBN 0-8069-3673-8

Pocket Puzzlers:
Lateral Thinking Puzzles

Paul Sloane

Des MacHale

Sterling Publishing Co., Inc. New York

Contents

The Puzzles

The Clues

The Answers

Index

The Puzzles

Angry Response

A man called his wife from the office to say that he would be home at around eight o' clock. He got in at two minutes past eight. His wife was extremely angry at his late arrival. Why?

Picture Purchase

An art expert went to a sale and bought a picture he knew to be worthless. Why?

Complete Garbage

The garbage was emptied out of the cans and a man died. How?

UH...WANNA RUN THAT BY ME AGAIN?

PEARLY GATES

Alone in a Boat

Why are two little animals alone in a little boat in the middle of the ocean?

Strangulation

A famous dancer was found strangled. The police did not suspect murder. Why not?

Golf Bag

During a golf competition, Paul's ball ended up in a bunker inside a little brown paper bag that had blown onto the course. He was told that he must either play the ball in the bag or take the ball out of the bag and incur a one stroke penalty. What did he do?

Flipping Pages

Yesterday, I went through a book, which I had already read, in a peculiar manner. After I finished a page, I flipped to the next page, then rotated the book 180 degrees. After that page, I rotated the book 180 degrees and then flipped to the next page, rotated the book 180 degrees again, and continued in this fashion until I was done with the whole book. What was going on?

Leadfoot and Gumshoe

A woman is stopped for speeding. The police officer gives her a warning, but the woman insists that she be given a ticket and a fine, which she promptly pays. Why did she want the ticket and fine?

Man in Tights

A man wearing tights is lying unconscious in a field. Next to him is a rock. What happened?

Straight Ahead

When the Eisenhower Interstate Highway System was built, it was specified that one mile in every five must be absolutely straight. Why?

Motion Not Passed

A referendum motion was not passed. If more people had voted against it, however, it would have passed. How come?

Fired for Joining Mensa

Mensa is a club for clever people. Anne's employer has no anti-Mensa feeling, but has made it clear to her that if she ever joins Mensa she will lose her job. How come?

Russian Racer

At the height of the Cold War, a U.S. racing car easily beat a Russian car in a two-car race. How did the Russian newspapers truthfully report this in order to make it look as though the Russian car had outdone the American car?

Winning Numbers

I have on a piece of paper the winning numbers in next week's lotto jackpot. I am an avid gambler, yet I feel I have very little chance of winning. Why?

Waterless River

Now for a riddle: What has rivers but no water, cities but no buildings, and forests but no trees?

The Test

The teacher gave Ben and Jerry a written test. Ben read the test, then folded his arms and answered none of the questions. Jerry carefully wrote out good answers to the questions. When the time was up, Ben handed in a blank sheet of paper while Jerry handed in his work. The teacher gave Ben an A and Jerry a C. Why?

Six-Foot Drop

A man standing on solid concrete dropped a tomato six feet, but it did not break or bruise. How come?

Reentry

What took 19 years to get into itself?

Seven Bells

A little shop in New York is called The Seven Bells, yet it has eight bells hanging outside. Why?

Assault and Battery

John is guilty of no crime, but he is surrounded by professional people, one of whom hits him until he cries. Why?

Statue of an Insect

Why is there a commemorative statue of an insect in a little town in the state of Alabama?

MAYOR, YOU KNOW THAT STATUE FOR YOUR "AUNT"?...

Up in the Air

One hundred feet up in the air, it lies with its back on the ground. What is it?

Clean-Shaven

Why did Alexander the Great order all his men to shave?

Adolf Hitler

During the war, a British soldier had Adolf Hitler clearly in the sights of his gun. Why didn't he fire?

Unknown Recognition

I saw a man I had never seen before, but I immediately knew who he was. He was not famous and had never been described to me. He was not unusual nor doing anything unusual. How did I recognize him?

Fair Fight

A boxer left the ring after winning the world championship. His trainer took all the money and he never got a cent. Why not?

Riddle of the Sphinx

The Sphinx asked this famous riddle: What is it that goes on four legs in the morning, two legs in the afternoon, and three legs in the evening?

Unclimbed

Why has no one climbed the largest known extinct volcano?

Talking to Herself

A woman is talking sadly. Nobody can understand her, but a man is filming her intently. Why?

Rejected Shoes

A man bought a pair of shoes that were in good condition and that fit him well. He liked the style and they looked good. However, after he had worn them for one day he took them back to the shop and asked for a refund. Why?

The Late Report

A man and his wife went on vacation. Two months later, the man called the police to report the location of a body near the place where he had been on holiday. The police thanked the man and then asked why it had taken him two months to report the body. What was the reason?

The Stranger in the Bar

Two men went out for a drink together in a bar. One of them looked up, saw a tall, dark stranger looking like death and drinking soda water, and pointed him out to his companion. Startled and uneasy, the two men left and went to another bar some miles away. After a few minutes, they looked up and saw the same sad, pale stranger drinking soda water. Deciding to leave, they went to a third bar, which was empty except for a young couple. However, within a few minutes, the cadaverous man appeared and, in a slow, sad voice, ordered a soda water. Almost out of his mind, one of the men went over to him and said, "Who are you and what do you want?" What did the man answer?

Gertrude

When Gertrude entered the plane she caused her own death and the deaths of 200 people. Yet she was never blamed or criticized for her actions. What happened?

Mad Cow Ideas

In 1996, the British government was faced with the task of slaughtering many thousands of healthy cattle in order to allay fears over the disease BSE, or mad cow disease. What proposal did the government of Cambodia make to help solve the problem?

The Cabbie's Revenge

An American tourist in London took a taxi cab. When he reached his destination, the tourist paid the taxi driver the fare, but did not include a tip. The taxi driver was displeased and said something to the American that ruined his whole evening. The two men were strangers and had never met previously. What did the cabbie say?

Where in the World?

In what place would you find Julius Caesar, the biblical Rachel, King David, Pallas Athena (the Goddess of War), King Charlemagne, Alexander the Great, Queen Elizabeth I of England and Sir Lancelot all together?

Scout's Honor

A boy scout was anxious to win maximum points at his monthly inspection. However, despite his mother's best efforts, she could not remove some blue felt-tip marker stains from his hands. What did she do?

Price Tag

Many shops have prices set just under a round figure, e.g., $9.99 instead of $10 or $99.95 instead of $100. It is assumed that this is done because the price seems lower to the consumer. But this is not the reason the practice started. What was the original reason for this pricing method?

The King's Favor

When King Charles II of England visited a College at the University of Cambridge, he noticed a fine

COULDN'T WE INTEREST YOU IN THIS WALLET SIZE, SIRE?

portrait of his father, King Charles I, hanging in the Main Hall. He asked if he could have it, but the ruling body of the College was very reluctant to part with it. At last the King said that he would grant the College anything in his power if they would give him the portrait and that he would be very displeased and unhelpful if they declined this generous offer. The College elders accepted. What did they ask for in return?

Color-Blind

John was color-blind. Because of this affliction, he landed an important job. What was it?

Seaside Idea

A military commander during World War II was on leave so he took his children to the seaside for a day. Here, he got the idea he needed in order to successfully carry out his next assignment. What was the idea?

The Hammer

Adam was jealous of Brenda's use of a computer. He changed that by means of a hammer. After that, he could use the computer, but Brenda could not. What did he do?

Souper

A woman was at an expensive and prestigious dinner. The first course was soup. Halfway through the course, she called over a waiter and whispered in his ear. He brought a drinking straw which she used to finish her soup. The other guests were surprised at her actions, but she had a good explanation. What was it?

The Stranger in the Hotel

A woman was sitting in her hotel room when there was a knock at the door. She opened the door to see a man whom she had never seen before. He said,

"Oh, I'm sorry. I have made a mistake. I thought this was my room." He then went off down the corridor to the elevator. The woman went back into her room and phoned reception to ask them to apprehend the man, who she was sure was a thief. What made her so sure?

Buttons

There is a reason why men's clothes have buttons on the right while women's have buttons on the left. What is it?

Upstairs, Downstairs

In a very exclusive restaurant several dozen diners are eating a top-class meal upstairs. Downstairs, precisely the same meal is being served at the same number of empty places where there is nobody to eat it. What is going on?

Early Morning in Las Vegas

A gambler went to Las Vegas. He won on the roulette table, lost at blackjack and won at poker. When he went to bed in his hotel room, he carefully double-locked his door. At 3 a.m. he was

EXCUSE ME, SIR. YOU LEFT A CHIP RIDING ON "7 RED". IT'S NOW WORTH $500,000. (...hello? ... new spin ... 26 black...okay) ...UH... SORRY TO BOTHER YOU, SIR.

KNOCK KNOCK

RING

awakened by the sound of someone banging and rattling on the door of his room. What did the person want and what did the gambler do?

Inspired Composition

A composer of music sat looking out of a window, hoping for inspiration. Suddenly something he saw provided him with the opening theme for a new work. What did he see?

Large Number

Assume there are approximately 5,000,000,000 (5 billion) people on earth. What would you estimate to be the result, if you multiply together the number of fingers on every person's left hands? (For the purposes of this exercise, thumbs count as fingers, for five fingers per hand.) If you cannot estimate the number, then try to guess how long the number would be.

Inner Ear

An insect flying into a girl's ear terrifies her. Her mother rushes the girl to the doctor, but he is unable to remove the insect. Suddenly, the mother has an idea. What is it?

The Single Flower

A woman was shown into a large room which contained over a thousand flowers. She was told that all but one of the flowers were artificial. She had to identify the real flower, but she could not examine the flowers closely nor smell them. She was alone in the room. What did she do to identify the single flower?

Unseen

As far as it is possible to ascertain, there is one thing which only one man in recorded history has not seen. All other men who have sight have seen it. The man was not blind and lived to a ripe old age. What was it that he never saw and how come?

The Champion's Blind Spot

At the dinner to celebrate the end of the Wimbledon tennis championship, the men's singles winner turned to the man next to him and said, "There is something here which you can see and all the other men can see but which I cannot see." What was it?

The Task

Several people are waiting to perform a task which they usually do by themselves very easily. Now, however, they are all in need of the services of someone who usually performs the task only with difficulty. What is going on?

WALLY Test

From the World Association for Learning, Laughter, and Youth (WALLY) comes another quickfire WALLY test. It consists of mean questions designed to trip you up. Test your wits now by writing down the answers to these questions. You have two minutes to complete the test.

1. There were eight ears of corn in a hollow stump. A squirrel can carry out three ears a day. How many days does it take the squirrel to take all the ears of corn from the stump?

2. Which triangle is larger—one with sides measuring 200, 300 and 400 cm or one with sides measuring 300, 400 and 700 cm?

3. How far can a dog run into a wood?

4. Which of the following animals would see best in total darkness: an owl, a leopard, or an eagle?

5. What was the highest mountain in the world before Mount Everest was discovered?

6. Where are the Kings and Queens of England crowned?

7. If the Vice-President of the USA were killed, who would then become President?

8. Which candles burn longer—beeswax or tallow?

9. A farmer had 4 haystacks in one field and twice as many in each of his other two fields. He put the haystacks from all three fields together. How many haystacks did he now have?

10. What five-letter word becomes shorter when you add two letters to it?

11. Which weighs more—a pound of feathers or a pound of gold?

12. What has four legs and only one foot?

Answers, page 93

What a Jump!

A man jumped 150 feet entirely under his own power. He landed safely. How did he do it?

The String and the Cloth

A man lay dead in a field next to a piece of string and a cloth. How did he die?

A Riddle

Four men sat down to play.
They played all night till break of day.

They played for gold and not for fun,
With separate scores for everyone.

When they came to square accounts
They all made quite fair amounts.

Can you this paradox explain?
If no one lost, how could all gain?

The Animal

At the Carlton Club, Alan Quartermaine was telling one of his stories. "When the animal emerged from the lake I could see that its four knees were wet," he said. Marmaduke, who had walked into the room at that very point, then interrupted, "I know what kind of an animal that was." How did he know and what kind of animal was it?

Bad Impression

A man entered a city art gallery and did terrible damage to some very valuable Impressionist paintings. Later that day, instead of being arrested, he was thanked by the curator of the art gallery for his actions. How come?

Escape

A man was trapped on an island in the middle of a large and deep lake. He could not swim and had no boat or means of making one. He waited desperately for help, but none came. Eventually he managed to escape. How?

Poisoned

A man is found dead in a locked room. He has died of poisoning and it looks like suicide. No one was with him when he took the poison. But it was, in fact, murder. How come?

Failed Forgery

A master forger forged a US $100 bill. The bills he made were perfect copies of the original in every detail, yet he was caught. How?

Apprehended

Some time ago a burglar ransacked a house in the middle of the night and left without anybody seeing him. Yet the police picked him up within a few hours. How did they trace him?

The Metal Ball

At the beginning of his act, a magician places a solid metal ball, 4 inches in diameter, on a table and places a cover over it. At the end of his act when he lifts the cover, the ball has disappeared. How?

One Croaked!

Two frogs fell into a large cylindrical tank of liquid and both fell to the bottom. The walls were sheer and slippery. One frog died but one survived. How?

COME ON — I'LL JUMP IF YOU DO.

ACME LIFE PRESERVER

Light Years Ahead

If you could travel faster than the speed of light, then you could catch up with the light which radiated from your body some time ago. You would then be able to see yourself as you used to be when you were younger. Although faster-than-light travel is impossible, at least at this time, how can we catch up with the light that we radiated earlier and see ourselves directly—as we used to be? (Such captured images as photographs, movies, and videotape do not count.)

The Newspaper

Jim and Joe were fighting, so their mother punished them by making them both stand on the same sheet of yesterday's newspaper until they were ready to make up. She did this in such a way that neither of the boys could touch the other. How did she manage to do this?

Unspoken Understanding

A deaf-and-dumb man went into a subway. He walked up to the cashier's booth and gave the cashier a dollar. The subway tokens cost 40 cents each. The cashier gave the man two tokens. Not a word was said, nor any sign given. How did the cashier know that the man indeed wanted two tokens?

His Widow's Sister

It was reported in the paper that Jim Jones had married his widow's sister. How did he do this?

Light Work

There are 3 light switches outside a room. They are connected to three light bulbs inside the room. Each switch can be in the on position or the off position. You are allowed to set the switches and then to enter the room once. You then have to determine which switch is connected to which bulb. How do you do it?

What a Bore!

An office worker has a colleague in her office outstaying his welcome. She can see that he is not inclined to leave any time soon. Concerned about his feelings, how does she manage to get rid of him without offending him?

Soviet Pictures

During the dark days of the Soviet Union, purges took place following which experts in photography would doctor photographs to remove individuals who had been purged. How was one expert caught?

Penniless

A struggling author receives a present of $2,000 from a lady admirer. He does not tell his wife about this cash gift, although she has shared all his trials and is very supportive. How did she find out that he had received the money?

The Deadly Suitcase

A woman opened a suitcase and found to her horror that there was a body inside. How had it got there?

Unknown Character

A recluse who had lived for many years in a small community was charged with a serious crime. He knew nobody in the area. Whom did he call as a character witness?

...BUT, MR. SOCKY, YOU ADMIT YOU WERE BLINDED BY A SHOE THE WHOLE TIME...

Gasoline Problem

A man's car runs out of gasoline. His car tank holds exactly 13 gallons. He has three empty unmarked containers which can hold 3 gallons, 6 gallons, and 11 gallons. Using only these containers at the gas station, how can the man bring back exactly 13 gallons? He is not allowed to buy more than 13 gallons and dispose of the extra.

Poison Pen

A woman received a very nasty, anonymous letter containing threats and allegations. She called the police and they quickly found out who had sent it. How?

The Music Stopped Again

When the music stopped, he died very suddenly. How?

Disreputable

A man was born before his father, killed his mother and married his sister. Yet he was considered normal by all those who knew him. How come?

Personality Plus

An agency offered personality assessment on the basis of handwriting. How did an enterprising client show that the operation was unreliable?

Gambler's Ruin

Syd Sharp, a first-class card player, regularly won large amounts at poker. He was also excellent at bridge, blackjack, cribbage, canasta, and pinochle. Joe, on the other hand, was terrible at cards; he could never remember what had gone before or figure out what card to play next. One day, Joe challenged Syd to a game of cards for money. Over the next couple of hours, Joe proceeded to win quite a large amount from Syd. How?

The Coconut Millionaire

A man buys coconuts at $5 a dozen and sells them at $3 a dozen. As a result of this he becomes a millionaire. How come?

BONK

IDEA

HEY! THIS'LL MAKE ME A MILLION!

The Clues

Angry Response

She was angry because he was late.

They had no particular appointment at eight o'clock.

Picture Purchase

He was honest and there were no crooked motives involved.

He did not intend to take any action to make the picture more valuable.

He would not have bought the picture if it had been rolled up.

Complete Garbage

If the garbage had not been emptied, he would have lived.

He was poor and tired.

He died a violent death.

Alone in a Boat

They were deliberately cast adrift from a famous boat.

The animals can sometimes offend the senses.

Strangulation

She was strangled to death with a scarf.

No dancing was involved.

She should not have been in such a hurry.

Golf Bag

Paul removed the bag without touching it.

He did not deliberately set fire to the bag since that would have incurred a penalty.

He indulged in a bad habit.

Flipping Pages

I did this deliberately in order to produce a specific result.

I could do this only in certain places.

I should have gotten permission from the publisher first.

Leadfoot and Gumshoe

She and the police officer were strangers and she was not trying to help or impress him.

She was acting from high moral principles, and was also protecting someone's reputation.

Man in Tights

He was knocked out by the rock, but it did not touch him.

He was involved in many dangerous adventures.

He was a well-known sight in his tights.

Straight Ahead

It was not done for economic reasons.

The straight miles make no difference to traffic conditions.

The straight miles were designed for use in extreme circumstances.

Motion Not Passed

Many people voted for the motion, and the poll was performed correctly according to the rules.

If a few more people had voted against the motion, it would have been passed. If many more people had voted against it, then it would have been rejected.

Fired for Joining Mensa

Anne's employers would not have objected to her joining any other organization.

She was employed in an administrative position, she did her job well, and her employers were pleased with her.

If she had joined Mensa, there may have been a conflict of interest.

Russian Racer

The papers reported accurately, but put the most positive light on the Russian car's performance and the most negative on the American car's.

The papers did not report how many cars raced.

Winning Numbers

If I participate, I will have the same chance as everyone else.

I am in no way prohibited from playing or winning.

The piece of paper has next week's winning lottery numbers on it. It also has last week's winning numbers.

Waterless Rivers

This is not a physical place.

It has mountains, but you could walk over them easily.

The cities, forests, mountains, and rivers are real places on planet Earth.

The Test
Each boy deserved the grade he was given.
There was something unusual about the test.
Jerry was not as diligent as he should have been.

Six-Foot Drop
The tomato fell six feet.
It was a regular tomato.
The man was fast.

Reentry
It is popular.
It is a collection.

Seven Bells
The shopkeeper could easily change the sign,
but chooses not to do so.

Assault and Battery

John is healthy.

The person who hits John does it to help him.

It is a common occurrence.

Statue of an Insect

The insect had caused a big problem.

The town's prosperity depends on agriculture.

The insect's actions caused a change.

Up in the Air

It is small.

It does not fly.

Check your assumptions on every word of the puzzle!

Clean-Shaven

Alexander the Great was interested in military conquest.

He believed that clean-shaven soldiers had an advantage.

Adolf Hitler

It was the real Adolf Hitler, the one who led the German Third Reich.

Adolf Hitler was alive at the time, and the war still had much time to run.

The British soldier did not recognize Hitler. But it would have made no difference if he had.

Unknown Recognition

The man was physically normal and there was nothing abnormal about his appearance.

I am not related to him, but a relationship is involved.

Fair Fight

The boxer did not expect to collect any money.

The trainer collected a worthwhile sum for his efforts.

The boxer won fairly, but without throwing a punch.

Riddle of the Sphinx

The Sphinx had poetic license. Morning, afternoon, and evening are metaphorical rather than literal times.

Not all the legs are limbs, but they all support the body.

Unclimbed

It is not underwater—it is clearly visible aboveground. It would be very difficult to climb.

Talking to Herself

The man was recording something for his archives.

She held a unique distinction.

Rejected Shoes

The shoes fit him comfortably, but there was something uncomfortable about them.

They were made of different material from his other shoes.

They were fine when worn outside, but not when worn inside.

The Late Report

The man was not involved in any way in the death of the person whose body he had reported.

The man had not noticed the body earlier, but did later.

The Stranger in the Bar

The two men were drinking beer while the stranger was drinking soda water.

The two men hadn't noticed the stranger outside the bars, but there was a connection between them and the stranger.

Gertrude

Gertrude caused a mechanical failure in the plane.

It was a jet aircraft.

Mad Cow Ideas

The Cambodian government suggested a way for Britain to get rid of the suspect cattle without risking that the cattle would eventually be eaten.

The suggestion involved the eventual death of the cattle in a way that would help solve a Cambodian problem.

The Cabbie's Revenge

The cabbie did not insult the American. He did not make any personal or nationalistic comment.

The cabbie gave the American a piece of factual information which the American did not want to hear. (We cannot tell you exactly what the cabbie said because it might ruin an evening for you too!)

The location to which the American was driven by the cabbie is important.

Where in the World?

Their images are found together in one common place.

They are found on something which is in common use and has been for many years.

They are used in a form of game.

Scout's Honor

She sent him to the inspection with the marks still on his hands.

She ensured that the marks would not be seen.

Price Tag

A price set at 5 cents, or even 1 cent, under a round dollar amount means that a customer would be entitled to change from a bill.

Smart shopkeepers were trying to protect themselves from losses.

The King's Favor

In a way, the King got what he wanted and the College got what it wanted.

The King took the portrait along with him when he left Cambridge.

No copy was made.

Color Blind

He was employed by the military.

He could see things other people found difficult to see.

Seaside Idea

He was a senior officer in the Royal Air Force.

He and his children threw stones into the sea.

The Hammer

Adam did not use the hammer on the computer. The computer was undamaged.

Brenda had a disability.

Souper

She was perfectly capable of consuming the soup with a spoon. There was nothing wrong with the soup.

Something happened halfway through the course which caused her to want to use the straw.

The Stranger in the Hotel

Hers was a single room.

There was nothing unusual about the man's appearance or bearing. The woman made a deduction based on what he said.

Buttons

This is not a fashion issue. It has to do with right- and left-handedness.

When buttons first came into use, it was the better-off who used them.

Upstairs, Downstairs

The restaurant is in an unusual location.

Early Morning in Las Vegas

The person who banged on the door was not a hotel official, nor a police officer or other such authority.

The gambler was not in danger.

Inspired Composition

He saw something which made no sound but which suggested a tune.

He saw some creatures at rest.

Large Number

The answer can be quickly and accurately deduced.

Think about the effect of actually multiplying the number of fingers on the left hands of all the people in the world, one after another.

The calculation might start $5 \times 5 \times 5 \times 5 \times 5 \times 5 \times 5 \times 5 \times 4 \times 5 \times 5 \times 5 \times 5 \times$ ...and so on.

Inner Ear

The mother lures the insect out of her daughter's ear.

The Single Flower
She got some help.
No other person was involved.

Unseen
It is known that this man led a secluded life.
Other men, even those blind from birth, would hear and touch this thing, but this man never heard or touched it.

The Champion's Blind Spot
The winner had perfect eyesight and could see as well as any other person there, but nonetheless, they could see something he could not see.
He could not see something relative to him which others could see relative to them.
If the winner had lost a game, then he could not make this claim.

The Task

The person who is performing the task has a disability.

Circumstances have changed so that the person's disability gives him an advantage over the others.

What a Jump!

He was an athlete.

He did not use any extra source of power but did use special equipment.

This happens regularly in a certain sporting event.

The String and the Cloth

He died an accidental death.

He had been holding the string.

It was a windy day.

A Riddle
They played seriously and each did his best.
Each man came out ahead.
No one joined their group.

The Animal
Marmaduke was able to deduce what the animal was from Alan Quartermaine's statement alone.
Only one animal has just four knees.

Bad Impression
He deliberately sprayed water over the paintings. This damaged them.
He was not unstable, deranged, or malevolent. He acted out of good intentions.

Escape
He did not attract or receive help in the form of a boat or a plane. He crossed the lake under his own power.
He was lucky to have found shelter.

Poisoned

The man was trying to gain sympathy. He was deceived.

The man wrote a suicide note and then deliberately took an overdose.

He did not intend to die. He expected to be rescued.

Failed Forgery

The paper he used was perfect. The color, texture, and watermark were perfect.

His copy was accurate in every way, yet the bills he made had an error that made them easily identifiable as forgeries.

Apprehended

The burglar left no clues inside the house.

The incident took place in the middle of winter.

The Metal Ball

The magician need not do anything to make the ball vanish.

He carefully makes and stores the ball before his act.

One Croaked!

The frogs were physically identical. One managed to survive the ordeal because of the result of its actions.

The nature of the liquid is important.

Light Years Ahead

There is a way in which we can see the light which we radiated and therefore an image of the way we were.

It is a common experience to view this image.

The Newspaper

Jim and Joe were normal boys aged seven and eight.

They both stood on the same sheet of newspaper, but, try as they might, they could not touch or even see each other without leaving the newspaper.

Unspoken Understanding
The man did want two tokens, and the cashier was able to correctly deduce this.

Nothing was written or signaled.

His Widow's Sister
When Jim Jones died, his wife became a widow.

No bigamy is involved and no life after death.

He had married his widow's sister quite legitimately.

Light Work
With just two bulbs and two switches, it would be easy.

Light bulbs give out light. What else do they do when they are switched on?

What a Bore!

The woman arranges an interruption, but no one else is involved.

She enjoys the advantages of modern technology.

Soviet Pictures

A fault was found in the photograph that proved it had been tampered with.

A fault was discovered by a count.

Penniless

The author did not know the identity of the lady admirer.

His wife was not jealous or concerned about the gift.

The Deadly Suitcase

The body was that of a child who had died accidentally through suffocation.

The woman was poor and had tried to save money.

Unknown Character

He called someone who did not know him.

By calling this person he hoped to prove that he was not a bad character.

Gasoline Problem

No complex mathematical combinations are needed to solve this one.

Poison Pen

They examined the letter very carefully.

The letter came from a pad of writing paper.

The Music Stopped Again

This has nothing to do with tightrope walkers!

A game was taking place. It involved music.

Disreputable

This is really three puzzles in one.

He was born after his father was. He did not murder his mother. He did not commit incest.

Personality Plus

The client submitted handwriting tests. He then simply showed that the assessments were incorrect.

Gambler's Ruin

They played cards, but Joe chose a game that suited him better than it suited Syd.

Syd had a handicap at this particular child's game.

The Coconut Millionaire

He lost money on every coconut he sold.

He did not make money by any related activity.

The Answers

Angry Response
The man had said he would be home at 8:00 P.M
He arrived the following morning at 8:02 A.M.

Picture Purchase
The picture was worthless, but it was in a fine
frame that he intended to reuse.

Alone in a Boat
The two animals were skunks that had been
ejected from Noah's Ark because of the stench
they were causing.

Strangulation

The famous dancer was Isadora Duncan, who was strangled when the long scarf she was wearing caught in the wheel of her sports car.

Complete Garbage

The man was sleeping in a garbage can that was taken to the compactor.

Golf Bag

To deliberately ignite the paper bag would be to interfere with his lie and incur a penalty. So while he pondered the problem he smoked a cigarette. He discarded the cigarette onto the bag and it burned. No penalty was incurred.

Flipping Pages

I was photocopying the book.

Leadfoot and Gumshoe

The woman is the wife of the chief of police. In

order to avoid any impression of favoritism she accepted the ticket and paid the fine.

Man in Tights

The man was Superman. He was lying next to a block of kryptonite, the one thing that could knock him out.

Straight Ahead

The straight sections were specified so that they could be used as aircraft landing strips in case of war or emergency.

Motion Not Passed

Although 35% of the people voted for the referendum motion and 14% against, there were not enough votes overall for a quorum to be reached. It needed 50% of the population to vote in order for the results to be valid. If another 1% had voted against the motion, it would have carried.

Russian Racer

The Russian newspaper reported (correctly) that the American car came in next to last while the Russian car came in second.

Waterless Rivers

A map.

The Test

The final instruction in the test was to ignore all the previous questions. The teacher had repeatedly told the students to read over the entire exam before beginning. The test was given to see how well the pupils could follow instructions.

Statue of an Insect

The insect is the boll weevil, which wreaked havoc with the local cotton crop. As a result, many of the farmers switched to growing peanuts—and became very rich when peanut prices rose.

Fired for Joining Mensa

Anne works for Mensa in the administration of admission tests. Under Mensa's constitution, no member can be an employee.

Six-Foot Drop

He caught it just above the ground.

Seven Bells

It was originally a mistake, but the shopkeeper found that so many people came into his shop to point out the error that it increased his business.

Reentry

The Guinness Book of Records, after 19 years of publication, became the second-best-selling book of all time and therefore got into itself.

Assault and Battery

John is a newborn baby. The doctor slaps him to make him cry and use his lungs.

Up in the Air

A dead centipede!

Clean-Shaven

Bearded men could be grabbed by the beard in close combat.

Adolf Hitler

This apparently true incident took place during the first World War when Adolf Hitler was a private in the German army. He was wounded and the British soldier thought it would be unchivalrous to kill him.

Winning Numbers

One has to choose six numbers from 60 for the

lotto jackpot. My piece of paper contains all 60 numbers, so it must contain the winning numbers.

Fair Fight

The boxer was a dog that had just won the championship at a dog show.

Unknown Recognition

He was the identical twin brother of someone I knew well. I had heard of him but had never met him before.

Riddle of the Sphinx

The answer is man, who crawls on all fours as a child, walks on two legs as an adult, and uses a walking stick in old age.

Unclimbed

The largest-known extinct volcano is Mons Olympus on Mars.

Talking to Herself

The woman was 87. The language she was speaking was dying out and she was the last person to know it. The man was an academic, who filmed her to record the language before it was lost forever. (This puzzle is based on the true story of Dr. David Dalby's filming the last woman to speak the African language of Bikya.)

The Unlucky Bed

Every Friday morning, a cleaning woman comes to the ward with a vacuum cleaner. The most convenient electrical socket is the one to which the patient's life support machine is connected. She unplugs this for a few minutes while she does her work. The noise of the vacuum cleaner covers the patient's dying gasps. The cleaner reconnects the machine and goes to the next ward. (Although this story was reported as factual in a South African newspaper, it is almost certainly an urban legend.)

Missing Items

The 10-year-old boy has kneecaps, which babies do not have. These develop between the ages of 2 and 5.

Once Too Often

Voting twice in the same election is electoral fraud—a serious offense.

Noteworthy

A burglar had broken into the woman's house and taken all her savings. In trying to collect the last bill that was stuffed into a jar, he tore it in half. She reported the incident to the police, and then took the half of the bill to her bank. They told her that a man had been in that morning with the matching half!

Rejected Shoes

The man found that the synthetic shoes generated a buildup of static electricity when he wore them around his carpeted office. He constantly got electric shocks, so he rejected them and went back to his old leather shoes.

Slow Drive
The man was moving. He was a beekeeper. In his car he had a queen bee. His swarm of bees was flying with the car to follow the queen bee.

The Late Report
The man saw the body in the background on one of his holiday photographs. It was two months before the film was developed.

The Stranger in the Bar
He said, "I am the taxi driver who has been driving you from bar to bar!"

Gertrude

Gertrude, a goose, had been sucked into a jet engine.

Mad Cow Ideas

The Cambodian Government suggested that the cattle be sent to Cambodia and allowed to wander their fields to explode the many mines left over from their wars.

The Cabbie's Revenge

The American was going to a performance of the famous Agatha Christie play *The Mousetrap*. The taxi dropped him outside the theater. The spiteful taxi-driver said "X did it," where X was the name of the murderer in the play. (We cannot state here X's name or we might ruin your future enjoyment of the play!)

Where in the World?

On a pack of playing cards. The original designs for the Kings, Queens and Jacks are based on these characters.

Scout's Honor

She covered the stains with a bandage strip. Nobody would remove it to check whether he had a cut.

Price Tag

The practice originated to ensure that the clerk had to open the till and give change for each transaction, thus recording the sale and preventing him from pocketing the bills.

The King's Favor

The College asked the King to return the painting in six months. Since this was clearly in his power he agreed.

Color-Blind

John was employed by the Air Force during wartime to detect camouflaged enemy positions from aerial photographs. Camouflage is designed to fool people with normal vision. People who are color-blind are much better at spotting differences in the texture and shading of landscape.

Seaside Idea

As he watched his children skimming stones on the water he got the idea for the famous bouncing bombs used by the "Dam Busters" in their raid against German dams. The bombs bounced along the surface of the lakes before hitting the dams and flooding large industrial areas.

The Hammer

Brenda was blind and she depended on her Braille manual when using the computer. Alan flattened the pages with a hammer.

Souper
Her contact lens had fallen into the soup and she wanted to retrieve it.

The Stranger in the Hotel
She reasoned that if it had really been his room he would not have knocked at the door but used his key. (She was on a corridor of single rooms, so it was unlikely he was sharing.) In fact, he knocked in order to check whether anyone was in before using a pass key to enter and burgle rooms.

Buttons
Most people are right-handed and find it easier to fasten a button which is on the right through a hole which is on the left. This is why men's buttons are on the right. When buttons were first used it was the better-off who could afford clothes with buttons. Among this class the ladies were often dressed by maid-servants. The servant would face the lady and so it was easier for right-handed servants to fasten buttons which were on the lady's left.

Upstairs, Downstairs

It is the First Class restaurant on a luxury ocean liner. Upstairs is out on deck. If it rains the entire company transfers downstairs and takes up where it left off.

Early Morning in Las Vegas

He had played poker in his room with friends until 2 a.m. They had all had plenty to drink and he had failed to notice that one of his friends had fallen asleep behind his sofa. Later, the man woke up and rattled the door as he tried to get out. The gambler let him out.

Inspired Composition

He saw some blackbirds sitting on telegraph wires. Their positions indicated a melody line.

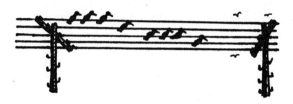

Large Number

The product of the number of fingers on the left hands of every person is zero. It only takes one person to have no fingers on his or her left hand for the product to be zero, because anything multiplied by zero is zero.

Inner Ear

She put the girl in a darkened room and placed a bright light near her ear. The insect emerged.

The Single Flower

She opened the window and a bee flew into the room. It settled on the one true flower.

Unseen

A woman! The man was Mihailo Tolotos, who was taken from his mother at birth and who spent all his life in the Greek monastery of Athos, where no females were allowed.

The Champion's Blind Spot
Every other competitor could see someone who had beaten them.

The Task
This is a true story that happened some years ago in New York during a power outage. A telephone exchange in a large apartment building was working on an independent power supply. Many people wanted to phone out, to reassure friends and relatives. They were helped in this by a blind man, who could do a much better job of dialing numbers in the pitch dark than any of them could.

What a Jump!
It was a ski jump.

The String and the Cloth
His kite had snagged across some electricity power lines. It was raining. He had been electro-

cuted. The cloth and string were the remains of the kite.

A Riddle
For the music they played,
Each band member was paid.

The Animal
Marmaduke knew that the only animal with four knees is the elephant.

Bad Impression
He was a firefighter who, in the course of putting out a fire, sprayed the room and paintings with water. He had indeed damaged the paintings, but saved them and others from complete destruction.

Escape
He walked over the frozen lake.

Poisoned

The man was separated from his wife but wanted to be reconciled. His nephew, and heir, suggested showing how distraught he was at the loss of his wife by staging a suicide attempt and taking an overdose. The nephew agreed to take the man's last, farewell letter to his wife so that she would rush round and save the man. Instead of doing so, the callous nephew stuck a stamp on it and posted it. By the time the wife reached her husband, he was dead.

Failed Forgery
He had copied a forged bill which itself contained a flaw.

Apprehended
It was during winter and the place was covered in snow. As the burglar backed his car to leave, he hit a snowbank and his number plate left a perfect impression in the snow.

The Metal Ball

The disappearing ball was a ball of frozen mercury, which was taken from a freezer. It melted during the course of the act.

One Croaked!

The frogs fell into a large tank of cream. One swam around for a while but then gave up and drowned. The other kept swimming until his movements turned the cream into knobs of butter, on which he safely floated.

Light Years Ahead

Yes—if you look in a mirror then you see light which left your body a finite time ago and has been reflected to reach your eyes. You see yourself as you were—not as you are!

The Newspaper

She slid the sheet of newspaper under a door. The boys stood on either side of the door but on the same piece of paper.

Unspoken Understanding

He gives the cashier four quarters, from which the cashier correctly deduces that the man wants two 40-cent tokens.

His Widow's Sister

Jim Jones married Ella in 1820. She died in 1830. In 1840 he married Ella's sister, Mary. She became his widow when he died in 1850. So in 1820 he had married his widow's sister.

Light Work

You set switches A and B on and switch C off. You wait a few minutes and then switch B off. You then enter the room. The bulb which is on is connected to A. The cold bulb which is off is connected to C. The warm bulb which is off is connected to B.

What a Bore!

She has a cellular phone in her pocket. Discreetly, she presses a button on it that causes it to give a test ring. She pretends that she has been awaiting an important call that she must take.

Soviet Pictures

In a group of ten Soviet officials photographed sitting around a table there were eleven pairs of feet underneath the table.

Penniless

The author's wife was the lady admirer. She had recently received a small legacy and did not want to offend him by offering him money directly.

The Deadly Suitcase

The body was that of the woman's son. They were flying to the U.S. to start a new life, but she did not have enough money for two airfares. She put him in a suitcase with tiny airholes. She did not know that the luggage compartment would be depressurized.

Unknown Character

He called the local sheriff, who had never heard of him. He used this as proof of his good character.

Gasoline Problem

The man uses the meter at the gas pump to measure out exactly 13 gallons. He puts 11 gallons in the large container and 2 gallons into one of the others.

Poison Pen

The sheet of paper on which the letter had been written had been taken from a writing pad. On the previous sheet, the culprit had written his address. This caused a slight impression on the sheet below. The address became visible when the policeman gently shaded the sheet with pencil.

The Music Stopped Again

He was an insect sitting on a chair seat during a game of musical chairs.

Disreputable

He was born in the presence of his father. His mother died at the birth. He became a pastor and married his sister to her husband.

Personality Plus

The man was ambidextrous. He gave two writing samples under different names—one written with his right hand and one with his left. The agency gave him two completely different personality profiles.

Gambler's Ruin

Syd Sharp was a first-class card player but he had a bad stutter. Knowing that Syd would be unable to respond fast enough to verbally announce the turning up of matching cards that the game's rules required, Joe challenged him to a game of Snap!

The Coconut Millionaire

The man is a philanthropist who bought great quantities of coconuts to sell to poor people at prices they could afford. He started out as a billionaire, but lost so much money in his good works that he became a millionaire!

WALLY Test Answers

Here are the answers to the WALLY test—get ready to kick yourself!

1. Eight days. Each day he takes out one ear of corn and two squirrel ears!

2. The first triangle is larger—one with sides measuring 200, 300 and 400 cm. The triangle with sides measuring 300, 400 and 700 cm has an area of zero!

3. Halfway—after that, it is running out of the wood.

4. In total darkness none of them could see a thing.

5. Mount Everest.

6. On the head.

7. The President would remain President.

8. No candles burn longer—all candles burn shorter.

9. He had one large haystack.

10. Short.

11. A pound of feathers weighs more than a pound of gold. Gold is measured in Troy pounds, which weigh less than the regular Avoirdupois pounds in which items such as feathers would be weighed.

12. A bed.

Rate your score on the following scale:

Number Correct	Rating
12 to 14	WALLY Whiz
8 to 11	Smart Aleck
4 to 7	WALLY
0 to 3	Ultra-WALLY

Index

Clue pages are in italics, answer pages are in bold face.